Frances Elizabeth Browne

Ruth

A sacred drama, and original lyrical poems

Frances Elizabeth Browne

Ruth

A sacred drama, and original lyrical poems

ISBN/EAN: 9783744781596

Printed in Europe, USA, Canada, Australia, Japan

Cover: Foto ©Thomas Meinert / pixelio.de

More available books at **www.hansebooks.com**

RUTH:

A

SACRED DRAMA,

AND

ORIGINAL LYRICAL POEMS,

BY

FRANCES ELIZABETH BROWNE.

NEW YORK:
PRESS OF WYNKOOP & HALLENBECK,
No. 113 Fulton Street.
1871.

PREFACE.

I HAVE been called upon to write a preface to this little volume.

With regard to the Drama, my idea of it was taken from a suggestion of our late celebrated English authoress, Mrs. Hannah More, in her introduction to her Sacred Dramas, that some other writer would carry out her desire, and make the admirable and exalted materials for poetry which the Bible contains the basis of other similar works.

This attempt, though weak and imperfect and very inferior to those of my great predecessor in this interesting path, may, I hope, be kindly received, as in some small degree drawing attention to the inexhaustible source from whence we derive every good and perfect gift.

A volume of my Lyrical Poems (as Mr. Longfellow was pleased to call them, and which received his unqualified approbation) were printed and so kindly received some years ago in Cambridge and Boston that two editions were sold out without the aid of a bookseller. Whether it was from their own merits, or from the kind patronage of my influential friends, I know not; but the fact of their being so quickly disposed of in this manner, encourages me to offer this later work to the public, with some other small pieces written since of a similar kind to my first, and also as many poems from the original publication as could well be included in a moderate-sized book.

How I have succeeded in this effort, I leave my readers to decide.

*

CONTENTS.

	PAGE
RUTH: A DRAMA,	5
STANZAS SUGGESTED BY A VIEW OF BOSTON FROM THE CUPOLA OF THE STATE HOUSE,	31
MOUNT AUBURN,	34
ON THE STORMY PETREL,	36
ON THE DEPARTURE OF A CLERGYMAN FOR EUROPE FOR THE BENEFIT OF HIS HEALTH,	39
ON THE DEATH OF HENRY CLAY,	42
ON THE MISSION TO INDIA,	44
LINES ON AN INCIDENT CONNECTED WITH THE BAPTISM OF TWENTY-FOUR CONVERTS,	47
LINES ON AN ACCIDENT IN PRINCE'S BAY, S. I.,	49
ON THE ASSASSINATION OF PRESIDENT LINCOLN,	51
ON PROFESSOR LOWE'S BALLOON ASCENSION, NEAR RICHMOND,	53
ON THE DEATH OF MY MOTHER,	55
ON THE LETTER O,	57
ON THE VISION OF ST. JOHN,	58
ON THE MIRACLE OF MOUNT HOREB,	61
BRAY HEAD, WICKLOW,	62
LINES TO ——,	64
THE MISSIONARY,	65
PAIN AND PLEASURE,	67
ON SEEING SOME CHILDREN BLOWING BUBBLES,	68

CONTENTS.

	PAGE
LINES SUGGESTED BY THE DISTRESS IN IRELAND, IN 1847,	69
SCENE AFTER A HURRICANE,	71
WELCOME SONG TO JENNY LIND,	74
ON MUSIC,	76
LINES TO A FRIEND,	78
THE WAGER,	80
A SKETCH.	82
L'INCONSTANT,	84
SELF-EXAMINATION,	85
LINES ON THE DEATH OF A YOUNG LADY,	87
ON THE DEATH OF THE DOWAGER LADY POWERSCOURT,	89
METRICAL LETTER TO MISS N——,	92
A SKETCH OF CONNEMARA,	94
TO A FRIEND,	97
TO A YOUNG LADY DURING SICKNESS,	99
LINES FOR AN ALBUM,	101
THE THREE AGES OF HUMAN LIFE,	103
LINES SUGGESTIVE OF THE HEROIC DEFENCE OF VERA CRUZ,	104
ON THE DEATH OF A FAVORITE CAT,	106
ON THE BAPTISM OF AN INFANT,	109
TO A FRIEND,	111
ON THE BIRTH OF AN INFANT,	112
TO ANNIE,	113
AN ACROSTIC,	114
HYMN,	115
ON THE ANNIVERSARY OF MY BIRTHDAY,	116
LINES TO AN OLD SCHOOLFELLOW,	120

SUBSCRIBERS.

THE UNDERSIGNED WERE AMONGST THE ORIGINAL SUBSCRIBERS TO MRS. BROWNE'S POEMS.

HARVARD UNIVERSITY.

Henry W. Longfellow. | Professor Norton.
Hon. Edward Everett. | C. Beak.

CAMBRIDGE.

Henry Dexter. | Mr. Lovering.
Mr. Felton.

BOSTON.

Hon. Abbott Lawrence. | Robert C. Winthrop.
Hon. Charles Sumner. | George Tickner.
Samuel Austin. | W. H. Prescott.
Bishop Eastburn. | Ives G. Bates.
Samuel Appleton. | J. D. Farnsworth.
William Appleton. | George T. Goddard.
Nathan Appleton. | H. G. Otis.
Henry G. Rice. | Alex. W. Vinton, D.D.
J. Quincy. | Franklin Haven.
James C. Dunn. | Oliver Wendall Holmes.
William Elliott. | A. Tewksbury.
N. L. Frothingham. | Wm. R. Lawrence.
A. A. Lawrence. | C. Frederick Adams, Jr.
Tyler Bigelow.

LIST OF SUBSCRIBERS.

CHARLESTON.

John T. Sargent.

SALEM.

Jared Sparks.
S. C. Phillips.
Thos. T. Stone.
H. Devereux.
Mrs. F. S. Carruth.
Mrs. Wiggin.
Mrs. Wm. W. Stone.
Mrs. J. Bigelow.
Mrs. E. Rollins.
Mrs. Geo. Darracott.
Mrs. T. H. Swett.

Miss A. Southwick.
Mrs. Shaw.
Mrs. Adams.
Mrs. Albree.
Mrs. Enoch Train.
Mrs. Gardner Brewer.
Mrs. R. Lawrence.
Mrs. F. B. Crowninshield.
Miss Tuckerman.
Mrs. R S. Fry.
Miss E. Wheelock.

PHILADELPHIA.

Joseph R. Chandler.
J. P. Durbin, D.D.
W. P. Wood.
M. N. Fay.
Lucretia Mott.
Mrs. E. Biddle.
Mrs. M. Patterson.
Mr. H. A. Grubb.
Mrs. Joseph Wood.
Mrs. Brock.
Mrs. Jane Sill.
Mrs. Frick.

Mrs. Isaac Elliott.
Mrs. Horace Binney.
Mrs. Cadwallader.
Mrs. Eleanor Glenholm.
Mrs. Goddard.
Mrs. N. Biddle.
Mrs. Robert Hare.
Mrs. Cope.
Mrs. J. Forsyth Meigs.
Mrs. Blaine.
Mrs. G. F. Lewis.
Mrs. Trevor.

Mrs. Lang.

LIST OF SUBSCRIBERS.

NEW YORK.

H. W. Bellows, D.D.
Rev. Samuel Osgood.
William Berrian.
B. F. Wheelwright.
B. G. Arnold.
George Newbold.

James Beatty.
P. A. Curtis.
F. H. Delano.
Robt. C. Woodbine.
Mrs. Kirkland.
Mrs. Oscar Coles.

Mrs. G. Warren.

BROOKLYN.

Mrs. Atkins.
Mrs. L. B. Wyman.
Mrs. Eastman.
Mrs. Ludlow Thomas.
Mrs. J. R. Gilmore.
Mrs. W. Halsey.
Mrs. C. Smith.
Mrs. A. H. Partridge.
Abbie L. Blake.
Mrs. H. Blake.
Mrs. Ibbotson.
Mrs. Lefferts.
Mrs. J. C. Dodge.
Mrs. Haviland.
Mrs. E. J. Lowber.
Mrs. Bainbridge.
Rev. Samuel Longfellow.
A. B. Sheldon.
Rev. Frederick A. Farley.
T. L. Mason.

Mrs. A. Claflin.
Mrs. Smith.
Mrs. Ives.
Mrs. Sanger.
Mrs. John Sneden.
Mrs. J. Cleveland.
Mrs. McMurray.
Mrs. L. Tappan.
Mrs. J. T. Moore.
Mrs. James Humphrey.
Mrs. Waring.
Mrs. Wyckoff.
Miss Newbold.
Mrs. Young.
Mrs. Bronson.
Mrs. Ryder.
Mrs. D. A. Kellogg.
Mrs. Lamont.
Mrs. H. M. Butler.
Mrs. Gray.

DRAMATIS PERSONÆ.

NAOMI,	Widow of Elimelech, an Israelite of Bethlehem-judah.
ORPAH,	Widow of Chilion, ⎱ Sons of Elimelech.
RUTH,	Widow of Mahlon, ⎰
RACHEL,	A Bethlehemite, an old friend of Naomi.
BOAZ,	A wealthy man of Bethlehem, a kinsman of Elimelech.
ELKANAH,	An old man, a nearer kinsman than Boaz.
AMINADAB,	Son of Rachel and a reaper in the fields of Boaz.
	Elders of Bethlehem.
	Female Singers, etc.

RUTH: A DRAMA.

Scene i.—*An Apartment in Moab.*

Present: Naomi *and* Orpah.

Orpah.—Mother, be comforted!
Naomi.—Console me not, my daughter; grief like mine,
If 't were to be impeded in its course
Or pent within my breast, would burst a heart
That's but too full already. Sympathy's the balm
Of which I stand in need; say, where is Ruth?
Bring her to me and we will weep together.
                                                [*Orpah goes.*
How cold a word is comfort to a heart
Just bleeding under fresh calamities;
And oh! compared to it, what luxury is sorrow!
Yet, great Dispenser both of good and evil,
It is not fretful murmurings and repinings
In which I would, in which I dare indulge.
Oh! be it far from me, a worm like me,
Presumptuously to question the decrees

Of thy unerring wisdom. Thou didst bless me
With a kind husband and two duteous sons;
Oh! then my cup of happiness was full,
Was full to overflowing—then our dwelling
Was as the fatness of the earth refreshed by dew
    from heaven.
Ah! happy, happy time passed in the bosom
Of my family, and with my own dear nation.
But 't is gone, for ever gone!
All my misfortunes began with thine, my country,
Oh that with thine they might have had an end!
Vain wish, and worse than vain, the Lord who
    gave me
The blessings I enjoyed, had he not then a right
To take them from me? When he bestowed them,
'T was not for my deserts; when he withheld them,
He still in mercy left me more, more, much more
Than I for sin was worthy.
The God of Israel for some wise purpose
Sent forth a grievous famine through the land
Of His own chosen people, many of whom
Were forced by dire distress to quit their native
    homes
And seek their bread among their wealthier neigh-
    bors.
I and my family, among the rest, with sorrowing
    hearts

Bade a long, sad farewell to Bethlehem,
Our dear and happy home; and having heard
That corn was plentiful throughout the land of Moab,
Directed thither our slow and heavy steps,
While many a prayer we offered up to heaven
For mercy, for ourselves, and for our country;
Mercy, that noble attribute of God,
Was not withholden from our ardent cries.
The Moabites received us kindly and supplied our wants.
Cheered and encouraged, we with lighter hearts
And brighter hopes industriously labored.
Soon again peace filled our minds
And plenty crowned our board.
But ah! a greater, a severer trial than poverty or exile
Soon was doomed me. I lost my friend, supporter, comforter;
My guide, my partner, both in joy and grief,
My husband, my Elimelech.
His death was worthy of his virtuous life;
O God! preserve my children; O support my wife, he cried;
Then sinking back exhausted, scarcely seemed to breathe.
In dread suspense I watched his pallid face,

And wiped the death cold drops that gathered
    round his brow.
Awhile he lay quite motionless, then faintly whis-
    pered,
My beloved Naomi, God is the father of the
    fatherless
And husband of the widow—this thought, this
    firm belief
Dispels all fear and makes a death-bed happy.
Yes, I die, Naomi, but, O my dear one,
A little while, and we again shall meet
Where death shall never more divide us;
Till then, farewell—he ceased.
Without a sigh his spirit winged its flight
To Abraham's bosom and to Israel's God.
My sons, when they arrived at man's estate,
Selected wives, idolatrous Moab's daughters.
Ah, then indeed I felt my great misfortune,
In being exiled from my native country,
In all its genuine bitterness.
Mahlon espoused Ruth and Chilion Orpah;
But blind and needless were my anxious fears
Lest my dear children should renounce the faith
In which they had so carefully been nurtured.
Wise would it be in us, the frail weak creatures
Of an omnipotent, omnicient God,
To trust all matters, all events to our Divine
    Creator,

Since all things shall work together
For the good of them who love and honor him.
Orpah and Ruth both outwardly conformed
To the religion of their honored lords;
Orpah, I fear, but outwardly conformed;
Ruth, I had hoped, was inwardly impressed
With those blest principles which seemed
To influence and mark her actions.
Alas! poor Ruth! who now with tender love
Will guide, encourage, and direct thy steps
Toward saving knowledge and eternal truth,
Since my last hope on earth, thy Mahlon, is no
    more?
Chilion first followed his beloved sire,
Then ere I had recovered from that stroke
Mahlon too died—my earthly ties are broken,

       [*Ruth enters; they rush into each
       others arms and weep.*

RUTH.—Dear mother!
NAOMI.—Dear Ruth!

       [*Ruth leads her to a seat, and sits
       down by her; they remain some
       minutes without speaking.*

RUTH.—I hope you feel relieved, dear mother?
NAOMI.—Yes, my Ruth, I do; these tears relieve me.
Never since my last dread shock
These eyes had shed one tear; ah, my child,

How am I stricken; all who blessed me
Beneath this lower sky have soared beyond it
And left this world a desert. Had I the means,
My daughter, of keeping thee now, my only comfort,
To soothe and solace my declining years;
But no, it is impossible; return thou and thy sister
To thy father's house, whilst I will bend
My feeble steps back to my native country,
There to claim from generous pity
The little nature craves.

RUTH.—And canst thou bid me leave thee?
Or dost thou think so meanly of poor Ruth
As that she would forsake the aged mother
Of her sainted Mahlon? and did a thought
So base find entrance in my heart—
To seek my parent's dwelling would be vain
Without renouncing Mahlon's pure religion.
No! I will never leave thee while these hands
Can minister to thy necessities.
        [*Enter Orpah.*

NAOMI.—Thou comest opportunely, Orpah;
I was just disclosing the plan which I have formed
Of going back to my beloved country.
I have heard how that the Lord hath visited
His people, recalled his exiled chosen to their
    Canaan.

  And again hath blessed their victuals with increase,
  And satisfied their poor with bread.
  I am old and feeble, and what I want their charity
  Will give till death releases me from all my woes.
ORPAH.—Surely, mother, we will go also with thee.
NAOMI.—No, my child, why would you go?
  Why waste the morning of your lives
  On one who soon must drop into the grave
  And leave you in a land of strangers
  Without a friend or home? No! nature calls you
  To a happier duty. You yet are young
  And may form other ties, which death I hope
  Will not so prematurely dissolve like those of late.
  I have no other sons; alas, my children,
  I grieve on your account; the Lord hath stretched
  Forth his hand against me.
ORPAH.—Mother, since you desire it, I will leave you;
  But never, never shall I cease to think
  Of all the love and kindness you have shown me.
  Farewell! and may the God in whom you trust
  Always preserve you.
NAOMI.—Farewell, my daughter, and may the same
   Jehovah
  Deal graciously with thee, as thou didst ever
  With Chilion and with me.
ORPAH.—Farewell, dear Ruth!
RUTH.—Farewell, Orpah! the God of Israel bless thee.

NAOMI.—Thou see'st, dear Ruth, I have prevailed on
   Orpah;
   Do thou go also; let no fear on my account deter
     thee;
   Be assured my God will guide me safely.
RUTH.—He can, he will, yet hear my firm resolve:
   Where thou goest I will also go;
   Where thou lodgest I will also lodge;
   Where thou diest *I* will also die;
   Thy people I will love as mine;
   And thy God serve as my God.

SCENE 2.—*The road to Bethlehem. Naomi, supported by Ruth, is met by an aged female, who gazes earnestly at her and exclaims:*

RACHEL.—Is this, can this be Naomi?
NAOMI.—Oh! call me not Naomi,* call me Mara.†
   Ah! seest thou not how bitterly the Lord
   Hath dealt with me? when I departed hence
   My God had richly blessed me; I went out full,
   But am returning empty.
RACHEL.—Welcome, thrice welcome, to the heart of
   Rachel

---

* Naomi, in Hebrew, signifies happiness.
† Mara, sorrow.

Thou art and ever wilt be. Alas! I see too well
Thy altered fortune plainly depicted
In thy grief-worn countenance;
I also have a tale of woe to tell.

NAOMI.—Dear Rachel, are we both then sisters in calamity?
Time has indeed so altered your appearance
That even Naomi, your old friend and companion,
Can scarcely recognize you.

RACHEL.—My dearest Naomi, I fear to ask—Elimelech; your sons?

NAOMI.—Are all, I trust, in heaven, my Rachel.

RACHEL.—Ah! would we also were;—there is, there must be,
A happier Canaan than our promised land.
But say, my sister, on whose support thou leanest?
Thou hadst, I think, no daughter.

NAOMI.—I had not, Rachel; but no child could ever
Be more dutiful than Ruth has been to me!
And, in return, she is indeed the daughter
Of my love. She was once the wife,
The happy wife, of my beloved Mahlon,
And since the hour that took away my son
She has assiduously striven to comfort his poor mother,
Though I know her own heart was nigh breaking.

Rachel.—Daughter of Moab! know the prayers and
  blessings
  Of age and of misfortune; the God of Israel
    hears;
  He will reward thee richly.
Naomi.—But tell me, Rachel, in this our toilsome
  Pilgrimage, what trials have been thine?
Rachel.—Ah, Naomi! severe and deep ones, not alone
  Pain, or disease, or poverty, or death, but worse,
  Far worse than these, than all—unkindness
  And ingratitude from those whom I best loved.
  But my dear old friend, the night is fast approach-
    ing
  Let us haste, ere darkness close around us;
  This night at least you both shall pass with me,
  And both shall share the widow's cake and cruse.
  I have one son, my greatest earthly blessing; he,
    I know,
  Will be rejoiced to see his mother's valued friend,
  Come, let us hasten hither.
Naomi.—Oh, Rachel! from my heart I thank thee
    for thy kindness,
  And joyfully accept it, for I feel I greatly need
    repose.
  My body is fatigued, and O my mind
  Is quite bewildered with the recollections
  Which rush upon my soul!

Ah, Bethlehem! Bethlehem! since I last beheld
    thee,
What misery I have known! Yet to be permitted
To come and lay my aged bones within thee
Calls for my deepest gratitude;
But O, Elimelech—my children—my dear child-
    ren.
RACHEL.—They, they are blessed.
NAOMI.—Yes! my God I thank thee. Dear Rachel
    lead me in.

SCENE 3--HARVEST.

A Field: Ruth gleaning after the reapers.

[*Enter Boaz.*

BOAZ (*to the reapers*).
    The God of Harvest bless this fruitful field
    And bless the laborers in it!
FIRST REAPER (*Aminadab*).—And may he bless our
    master
    As he doth bless his servants.
BOAZ (*to 1st Reaper*).—Who is yon lovely damsel?
FIRST REAPER.—My lord, she is a Moabite, and hither
    came
    With the poor old Naomi, who has just returned

From sojourning in Moab, where she lost
Elimelech her husband, and her sons.
Ruth, the damsel's name, was wife to Mahlon,
Naomi's eldest son, and when her husband
Died, and left his widowed mother old, poor,
And helpless, this exemplary woman
At once resolved to cherish and console her,
Forsook her native land, and journeyed with
Her here, where now she strives by gleaning
To support her. My mother and Naomi
In early youth were friends; and Ruth and she
Abide with us until they can procure a better
  home.
BOAZ.—Oh, matchless force of conjugal affection!
Which even death has not had power to conquer.
Oh, virtuous Ruth; and fair as thou art virtuous!
A Moabite, thou mayest put to shame
Israel's most favored daughters!
For thee, Aminadab, thou and thy mother
Doubt not wilt receive a blessing from on high
For succoring the aged and the widow.
I now must do my part, and oh, how sweet the
  duty!
The strangers shall not want a friend
Whilst I have power to help them.
Meanwhile let them remain with you
Until I can resolve how best to serve them.

Let the damsel glean and gather freely,
And rebuke her not; and charge my reapers
That they treat her kindly as they hope
To gain their master's favor.
If she be wearied with the toil and heat,
Do thou assist her and see that she partake
Of the repast at noon.

    [*Boaz walks to another part of the field and addresses Ruth.*]

BOAZ.—Blessed be thou my daughter! go not hence,
But tarry with my maidens;
Take what thou wilt, and fear not a reproach.
The reapers I have charged to treat thee kindly
And at mid-day go and partake their meal.

RUTH.—Oh, my lord, how shall I find words to thank you
For all this goodness to a friendless stranger?

BOAZ.—No thanks are due to me, I but perform my duty.
The God of Israel, that God under whose wings
Thou now hast come to trust, commands us
To assist the stranger and the widow; but, my daughter,
I have heard of all thy filial duty to Naomi,
How for her sake thou hast renounced thy country
And come into a land where thou wast quite unknown.

My heart now pays its tribute to such virtue
And eagerly it prompts what duty offers.
RUTH.—My lord, what I have done deserves no praise.
I have no merit which can claim this kindness;
But gratitude to you, and to that God,
To whose interposition I alone can owe the favor
Thou hast shown me, will, I trust, prove
I was not unworthy. The God of Israel has long
Been my God; and his precepts, pure and holy,
As he is holy, declare he is the true God.
Oh that Moab would cease to worship Baal!
My heart bleeds for my country—shudders
To behold its blindness and idolatry.
But, alas! how can the God of Israel hear the prayers
Of one whose youth to idols was devoted?
Else how, my country, would I pray for thee!
BOAZ.—Daughter, the God of Israel is just as well as holy,
And merciful as just. Though thy youth
Has been indeed devoted to idolatry,
Thou worshipped in ignorance;
And, having done so, fear not that that just being
(Who is himself alone the source of knowledge)
Will e'er condemn thy ignorance as sin.
When light was given thee thou didst then

Embrace it; fear not, the mercy that has led thee
Hither will not refuse to listen to thy prayers.
BOAZ (*alone*).
What piety, simplicity, yet high-souled virtue
This Moabite displays! What modest dignity
The inward consciousness of rectitude imparts
To all her thoughts, and words, and actions;
What beauty, too, regardlessly possess'd!
Yes, lovely as she is, a mind like hers
Possesses too much value in itself
To cast a thought upon the form it animates.
How am I to act? the law of Israel
Would give this young and lovely Moabite
To age and to moroseness; the nearest kinsman
   of her husband Mahlon
Is old, stern, and ill-favored; yet he is rich
And powerful; and am not I as rich!
As powerful! and younger far than he is?
Yet 'tis my duty, and I will perform it,
To tell him of the treasure in his reach.
He may indeed refuse it, for to him
The Moabitish Ruth may not be pleasing,
And then, oh then, she is my own.
I am her next of kin; yet shall I owe to duty
What I would owe to love? No,
I will see her kinsman, and if, as I desire,
He should renounce her, I will endeavor

To gain her heart; and if, alas! I fail,
I will then purchase the land that was Elimelech's
And restore it to her and to Naomi,
Free and without conditions, and never
Shall she know the claim which I possess'd,
Or sacrifice I make. If her affections
Cannot be mine, my love is too sincere
To force her to be so against her own consent.
Ah, surely our all-righteous Judge,
Our Law-giver divine, is far too just
Ever to have design'd to authorize compulsion.
                                            [*Exit Boaz.*

SCENE 4.—*The road to the city of Bethlehem from the fields of Boaz. Ruth appears with the gleanings over her shoulder. Aminadab, the son of Rachel, awaiting her approach.*

AMINADAB.

Why tarriest thou? the day is waning fast
Thou virtuous daughter of a foreign land,
Oh let me bear thy burden—sweet the labor
                        [*takes her bundle of gleanings.*
When 'tis for thee I bear the fragrant load.
Why thou hast labored hard; thou hast at least
An ephah of fine barley in thy sling.

RUTH.

I had not gleaned the half of what thou see'st
But for the kindness of the generous Boaz,
Who bade his reapers strew the golden sheaves
Right in my path, as if 'twere accidental.
I heard him as I stopped behind a mow,
And bless'd him in my heart for his true goodness.

AMINADAB.

Oh, Ruth! no longer stoop to these mean labors,
But as my dear and cherish'd wife remain
At home with thy dear mother and my own,
And make our fireside happy.

RUTH.

Ah, no! Aminadab, my heart lies buried
In the cold tomb of my beloved Mahlon.
I love thee as a brother; feel the kindness
Thou and thy mother show'st to me and mine,
And the sweet pity which would take a stranger,
A desolate widow, to thy house and home.
But never can my heart respond to aught
But what's connected with my sainted Mahlon.
For that I followed his dear mother here;
And while I minister to her I feel
I still have something left my husband honor'd

For that I sought the God my Mahlon worship'd,
And left my country and its senseless idols.
No, no, Aminadab, seek out a virgin
Whose first pure love and heart may be thine own,
Then shall she cling to thee with such devotion
As clings poor Ruth to Mahlon's sainted shade.

AMINADAB.

Oh ! say not so, dear Ruth; no after love
Can this poor heart, this faithful bosom move.
Thee, it's first star of hope, its dream of joy
No future vision can its beams destroy.

SCENE 5.—*The barn-yard of the dwelling of Rachel.*

Present: RUTH, NAOMI *and* AMINADAB. *The latter, laying down Ruth's gleaning before Naomi, retires into the cottage.*

NAOMI.

Dear daughter, prop of my declining age,
Thou'rt kindly welcome to Naomi's sight;
Sole remnant of the dear familiar faces
Which smiled sweet love and peace in days gone
    by.
Where didst thou glean, my daughter ?   In

Whose fields hast thou pursued thy hard
But pious labors to support the poor
Dependent on thy duteous love? Surely
Some Israelite, whom Moses' spirit has
Moved to care for the widow and the
Stranger, must have increas'd thy store.

RUTH.

Yes! mother, yes! It was my hap to labor
In the smiling fields of a rich man
Named Boaz; and whilst I carefully
Pick'd up the scatter'd sheaves, he chanced
To walk forth in the morning air
To view the laborers gather in his harvest.
With what a graceful step and noble mien,
Such as they say Prince Abraham wore of old,
He moved and spoke. His eagle glance
Soon noted my foreign garb and accent,
And he turn'd to our kind friend, Aminadab,
To ask my name and country. When he
Had told him all, he look'd upon me,
And, with a beaming smile so like
My sainted Mahlon's, laid his hand
Upon my head and bless'd me
In the name of Israel's God.
He told me, too, never to quit his fields
Nor to bring aught with me for my

Refreshment, but to eat and drink
With his young men and maidens
Till the end of all his harvest.

NAOMI.

'Tis well, my daughter. See they find thee not
In any other field.
Do thou his bidding, follow with his maidens
Where'er their master setteth them to reap—
He is a kinsman of the tribe of Judah.
Our holy law gives thee a powerful claim
On his protection. He loved thy husband,
And before our exile showed us much kindness;
And blessed be he of the Lord his God,
For shewing to the widow of his friend
The kindness which the dead no longer needeth.
The dreadful flood which made our smiling
Fields a barren desert, and forced so many
Families of Israel to seek subsistence
For their starving flocks through the
Surrounding countries, scarcely touched
His higher lands.
Since that time, like Abraham's,
His possessions have increased,
Till now he is reputed the most wealthy
Of Judah's prosperous tribe.

SCENE 6.—*The Gate or Court-house of the City of Bethlehem.*

Present: Ten Elders or Senators, forming a Quorum or legal court; BOAZ *and* ELKANAH, *the two kinsmen of Elimelech;* NAOMI *and* RUTH.

BOAZ.—Elders of Israel! Senators of Bethlehem!
  I have called you hither to claim your aid
  To enforce one of the laws which Moses gave our tribes.
  Elimelech of Bethlehem, a kinsman of my house,
  During the famine which ten years ago
  Laid waste our fruitful fields,
  Sought refuge in the land of Moab,
  Where he dwelt some time in peace and safety,
  There his sons, Mahlon and Chilion, took them Moab wives;
  He died an exile in that distant land
  And both his sons died also.
                          [Leading Naomi forward.
  His widow here I now present to you,
  Returned in her old age bereft of both
  Her husband and her sons, while all the land
  Which was Elimelech's and theirs, is now
  Annexed to that of their next kinsman.
  Naomi prays for her late husband's rights
  According to our just and sacred law!

NAOMI.—My lords, I beg your kind and gracious aid.
FIRST ELDER.—And thou shalt have it, thou afflicted woman!
Let the possessor of the lot pertaining
To Elimelech of Bethlehem, be called.
ELKANAH (*coming forward*).
Behold him here.
Elders! my father Simeon held the lot
Which was Elimelech's since that sad day
When famine forc'd our kinsman from his home;
Then it was worthless; Siddim's marshy vale,
Where my poor kinsman's patrimony stood,
Was subject to such storms at harvest time,
When Jordan's stream o'erflows,* that all his fields
Were inundated by the o'erwhelming flood,
And he with all his family obliged to fly
To Moab's nearest plains. Since my father's death
Left me the charge of these impoverished fields,
By ceaseless toil, by digging drains and building up
Embankments to keep the sea from rushing o'er the land,

---

* Jordan overfloweth all his banks all the time of harvest.—Joshua, c. iii. v. 15.
The vale of Siddim, which is the salt sea.—Genesis, c. xiv. v. 3.
This then was the lot of the tribe of Judah. Their south border was from the shore of the salt sea.—Joshua, c. xv. v. 1, 2.

And making Jordan's stream a whelming flood
To carry all before it, instead (as now it is)—
A welcome irrigation—I have succeeded,
With heaven's kind blessing on my humble labors,
In making it one of the finest lots of Judah's
    beauteous land.
I will redeem it at Naomi's hands for its full
    value,
And will give her what will make her widow'd
    age
Prosperous and even wealthy.

BOAZ.—Elkanah, thou wouldst thus indeed fulfill
A *part* of Moses' law, but not the whole!
For Naomi has not returned alone,
But was accompanied by Ruth of Moab,
The virtuous widow of her oldest son.
Ruth has renounced her country and its idols
To seek Naomi's God, the God of Israel.
Here she has toiled with sweet humility,
Tho' there she might have dwelt in ease and
    splendor.
Our law decrees that when a brother dies
He who would hold his heritage, must take his
    widow, too,
To be his lawful wife, and heirs be raised,
To keep each lot in its appointed tribe.
Wilt thou do this, Elkanah?

ELKANAH.—No! that I cannot do,
    Lest I should mar my own inheritance
    And bring disunion in my happy home.
    I honor Ruth's virtue and goodness, but
    I honor more my Hannah's long tried worth,
    My cherish'd wife, nor willingly would I
    Bring foreigners to rival the pure love
    I bear my children! Boaz, *thou* art free;
    Thou hast as yet, I think, no wife or children
    Whose jealousy this foreigner might raise;
    I know thou lovest Ruth! Think not Elkanah
    Will mar thy bliss; I heard thee when thou thoughtest
    No other ear but Israel's God's was listening!
    "Old, tho' I am," and stern," as thou didst think me,
    I honor'd thy resolve to keep God's law,
    And give the nearest kinsman and possessor
    Of the inheritance the right of *choice*,
    Tho' it might break thine heart! Like Abraham's,
    The sacrifice will not be needed! 'Twas to try thy faith;
    And thy loved Isaac, bound on heaven's high altar,
    Is now to be released and be thine own.
    She loves thee, too; I know it by her sighs
    And tearful trembling, lest *I* should claim her!

Boaz, take thou *my* rights unto thyself!
In true and solemn token that to thee
I give up *all* inheritance and Ruth,
I hereby draw my sandal from my foot
And give it to thee and thy heirs forever.

[*Gives Boaz his shoe.*

BOAZ (*to the Elders and people*).

Elders and brethren, ye are witnesses
That I have bought this day from Naomi
All that pertaineth to her husband's house,
Elimelechs, and Chilion's, and Mahlon's;
And Ruth, the Moabitess, have I bought
To be my lawful wife, to raise the name
Of her dead husband, Mahlon, in his place
Among his brethren.

THE ELDERS AND PEOPLE—We are witnesses.

[*Enter Chorus of women, led by Rachel.*

Sound the loud Timbrel in Bethlehem's gate,
With Cymbals and Psalt'rys the tidings relate;
The Moabite daughter, whose virtue we praise,
Has crown'd with her love our Naomi's last days.

Let the house of great Boaz receive thee with
    pride,
Thou hast come to our nation with God for thy
    guide;
Seven sons to Naomi could never impart
The joy thy affection has brought to her heart.

From thee shall the true house of Israel rise;
Thy sons shall be valiant, thy daughters be wise;
'Midst the princes of Judah their dwellings shall be,
And the blessing of Jacob descend upon thee.

STANZAS

SUGGESTED BY A VIEW OF BOSTON FROM THE CUPOLA OF THE STATE HOUSE.

From Albion's isle I come;
   I was born on a foreign strand,
Yet I love the Pilgrim's home,
   And am proud on this spot to stand.

O, much did I long to see
   The scenes of their bright career—
Of the good, the brave, the free—
   Of their toils and their triumphs here!

Canadian shores I've viewed;
   I have sailed on St. Lawrence tide;
On Quebec's fair plains I've stood,
   Where our British hero died.

But theirs was a brighter crown
   Than earth's highest honors yield—
A victory harder won
   Than the fame of the proudest field.

They scaled not the dangerous height
  Of a fort or a castle's brow,
But they gained heaven's regions bright,
  By virtue's steps below.

Their path was more dark and steep
  Than Wolfe's daring footsteps trod,
But it led o'er the stormy deep,
  To freedom, and fame, and God.

They fought not with bomb or shell,
  Artillery's dreadful rage,
Yet Satan's empire fell,
  And with sin fierce war they wage.

The sword of the Word of God
  They bore to a distant land;
Where no Christian's foot had trod
  They stood, a patriot band.

Their country was not of earth —
  As pilgrims they lived and moved;
They rejoiced in their heavenly birth,
  And they spoke of the land they loved.

They told the poor Indian, lost
  In ignorance dark as night,
Of the price his redemption had cost —
  Of Jesus, and heaven, and light.

They taught him that Jesus' command
  Was that wars and contentions should cease;
That his symbol in every land
  Was the olive-branch, whispering peace.

Americans! ye who delight
  In the fame of these heroes of old,
Beware how their precepts ye slight—
  More precious than silver and gold.

Let freedom to worship your God,
  Let peace, by your fathers bequeathed,
Your triumph at home and abroad,
  Round your star-spangled banner be wreathed!
  3*

MOUNT AUBURN.

Sweet Auburn! which with verdure and with bloom
Adorn the precincts of the darksome tomb,
Divests the grave of half its dread array,
Plants living flowers upon the lifeless clay,
Hallows the memory of the cherished dead,
And turns to balmy dews the tears we shed,
Accept a tribute from a stranger's pen,
Meet resting-place of brave and pious men!

There marble monument and sculptured bust
Seem to reanimate the silent dust,
Give to each grave a voice, whose thrilling tone
The sorrowing hearts of friends and kindred own!
Imagination revels in the scene,
And fills with fancied forms each alley green—
Hears Channing preach with eloquence divine—
Spurzheim philosophy's wise precepts join;
Heroes address their friends in martial strains
Tell them of Bunker Hill and battle-plains;
Others, who braved the dangers of the sea,
To serve their country and preserve it free,
The spangled banner o'er the waves unfurled,
The naval bulwarks of the Western world,

Now safely landed on a peaceful shore,
Where wars no longer rage, nor billows roar,
Still hovering round, may angels wings expand,
Be guardian spirits of their native land.

But see where yonder little cherub lies,
As if sweet sleep had gently closed her eyes!
One beauteous foot across the other thrown,
Calm she reclines, in infant grace alone.
While gazing on that face so sweet and mild
The parents still may dream they have a child;
For she, alas! so deeply cherished here,
She was their only one,—thus *doubly* dear!

Nor scorn we to appropriate a place
To yonder emblem of the canine race;
But honored still for ages yet to come
The faithful dog here guards his master's tomb!
In sculptured stone immortalized is he—
A noble tribute to fidelity!
Beside the friends in life he loved to guard,
In death he gains this justly earned reward.

Bright resting-place of faithful hearts and true,
Auburn! New England's pride and boast, adieu!

ON THE STORMY PETREL.

CALLED BY SAILORS MOTHER CAREY'S CHICKENS.

Bird of untiring wing,
    Whence dost thou come?
Bird of deep mystery,
    Where is thy home?

On the broad ocean wave
    How canst thou rest?
Where dost thou roost at night?
    Where build thy nest?

Land is too far from thee
    On every side,
Thousands of miles away
    Over the tide.

Yet dost thou carelessly
    Sport o'er the wave,
Fearless of finding
    A watery grave!

When the storm rages,
   And tempests beat high,
Still on the crests
   Of the billows you fly;

Sportively, joyously,
   Dart through the foam,
Still seem delighted
   O'er ocean to roam.

Bird of three elements,
   Air, water, earth,
Where dost thou rear thy young?
   Where hail their birth?

Is it on some lonely
   Rock in the sea,
Where human hand or foot
   Never may be?

Dost thou from such lone spot
   Launch o'er the flood,
Bringing along with thee
   Thy youthful brood?

Over the deep, deep sea,
   Like thee to fly,
Like thee to bring their young,
   Flutter—and die?

ON THE STORMY PETREL.

Bird of existence brief,
  Man is like thee,
Launching, he knows not where,
  O'er a wide sea;

Tossed on the billows
  Of life's stormy wave,
Restless as thou,
    Till he sinks in the grave;

But not like thee, poor bird,
  Never to rise!
Soon on the wings
  Of the spirit he flies—

Soars through eternal space,
  Ransomed and blest—
Mounts to heaven's utmost height!
  There is his rest.

ON THE DEPARTURE OF A CLERGYMAN FOR EUROPE FOR THE BENEFIT OF HIS HEALTH.

Go! beloved pastor, go!
   On thy steps may angels wait,
Guardians of God's saints below,
   May they watch thy future fate.

Whilst o'er ocean's billowy breast
   Thy trans-Atlantic wanderings lead,
Oh! may they lull each storm to rest
   And bid thy vessel safely speed.

Oh! may they waft refreshing gales,
   With strengthening power from spray and foam,
As on her course she calmly sails,
   And seeks my much loved English home.

But more than all, may gales of peace
   From Heaven's own shores thy bosom fill,
The graces of thy soul increase,
   Thy power to do a Saviour's will!

First stretched along broad Mersey's stream
    My native town will meet thy view,
Of England's merchant cities, queen—
    What noble docks, what shipping too!

What thousands crowd her busy quays
    And anxious scan each stranger's face,
With curious scrutinizing gaze,
    The features of some friend to trace.

While smiling at the busy scene,
    Across the water " Cheshire " lies,
Her waving fields, her lawns so green,
    Extend 'till " Cambria's " mountains rise.

My country! Oh! my feelings warm
    As thus I trace each well-known spot—
Unworthy of a human form
    Is that cold heart which loves thee not

Tho' in this world of chance and change
    Those shores I never more may see,
Yet in unfettered fancy's range,
    My honor'd friend, I go with thee.

Again I view the cloistered pile
    Within fair Cestria's* ancient walls
I tread the venerable aisle,
    And plainly on my ear there falls

---

* " Cestria," the ancient name for Chester.

ON THE DEPARTURE OF A CLERGYMAN.

The silvery chimes of sweet-toned bells,*
　　Along bright Deva's† "Wizard stream,"
Whose echo of that period tell
　　When life was yet a beauteous dream!

Tho' I may never trace again
　　The relics of "the Saxon age,"
The towers o'erlooking moor and glen
　　Where kings beheld their troops engage,‡

Yet thou wilt view the symbols fair
　　Of England's dawn and earlier day,
Wilt gaze on Cestria's walls so rare,
　　And in her antique temples pray.

Farewell! May health and peace be thine,
　　And temperate climes thy sinews brace;
Thy flock for thy return will pine,
　　And all thy wanderings fondly trace.

---

　*The bells of old St. John's Church, by the river side, are famous for their sweet silvery tones.

　† "Deva," the ancient name of the river Dee.

　‡ An old tower on the walls of Chester bears this inscription: "King Charles stood on this tower and saw his armies defeated on Rowton Moor."

ON THE DEATH OF HENRY CLAY.

Yes! Clay's bright course on earth is o'er
And "Ashland's Sage" is gone!
The dear old Patriarch is no more!
Mourn! sons of freedom, mourn!

Dear, patient sufferer! Thou didst long
Await thy heavenly change;
Now out of weakness thou'rt made strong,
Through brighter worlds to range.

He's gone to celebrate above
His country's festal day;
Oh! while that country's name ye love
Remember Henry Clay!

For half a century's rolling years
His talents were her pride;
When threat'ning clouds alarmed her fears,
His counsels aid applied.

He loved her with the purest love
A Patriot's bosom knows,
But all mankind his feelings moved,
For *all* that bosom glows!

Poor Afric's sons to him were dear,
And sympathy could wake,
And all his eloquence appear
For fallen Grecia's sake.

Virginia's "Mill Boy," thou didst soon
Thy true position claim!
Thy talents gain'd a brilliant noon,
Thyself a noble name!

Thy youthful sun, through fogs and clouds,
Arose with glittering light,
Dispersed the shades thy dawn enshrouds,
With intellectual might.

That name shall ever brightly shine
In History's glowing page,
With Washington shall proudly twine
The glories of their age!

ON THE MISSION TO INDIA.*

I stood amongst a list'ning crowd
Upon New England's hallow'd sod,
And whilst each head devoutly bow'd,
Before their Pilgrim Fathers' God,
I thought perchance their spirits near
Might hover o'er the sacred scene,
Rejoic'd to view the sheaves appear
Where their "seed-scattering steps" had been.

But who, but He who form'd the world,
And blesses those who sow in tears,
Who saw their flut'ring sail unfurl'd
With simple faith, but inward fears,
Who guided that lone "Mayflower's" track
To Massachusetts' shelt'ring Bay,
Who warded off each fierce attack,
From savage Indians, bent to slay!

Who fed and watched his little flock
In this dread wilderness afar!

---

* These lines were suggested by the farewell meeting in Park Street Church, Boston, on the occasion of the departure of the Rev. Dr. Scudder, Rev. Mr. Spaulding, etc., for Southern India.

O! who but "He," Salvation's Rock,
The Christian Pilgrim's guiding star,
Could ever dream that scenes like this
Would be the product of their toil!
To send forth harbingers of bliss
To distant India's burning soil.

Yet such it was! proud sceptic cease!
And doubt God's promises no more!
The Gospel of the "Prince of Peace"
Is borne from this to India's shore!
The little persecuted band,
The grain of mustard seed, so small—
Is now a tree, and fills the land,
And spreads its boughs to shelter all!

Aye! stretches o'er the distant main,
To grasp the world in its embrace,
To break sin's harsh and galling chain,
Where e'er it binds the human race!
Aye! soon shall every link be riv'n,
Forg'd by the powers of Hell combin'd!
To keep the fetter'd soul from Heav'n
And captive hold the human mind!

Think ye to see a Saviour come
With shining hosts reveal'd from Heav'n?

Not so, vain man! let pride be dumb,
Not such the symbols Christ has giv'n!
The "Leaven," the mustard seed so small,
The power of truth, the power of grace,
Soon shall the world before it fall,
And Satan's lying dreams give place.

Mahomet feels *his* kingdom shake,
Nor dares (as once) the sword to wave
In Christian blood, his thirst to slake,
And doom the "Heretic" a grave!
"Brahma" now totters on his throne,
Tho' victims still his course attend,
And the poor "Suttee's" piercing groan,
In flames and blood to Heav'n ascend.

China receives her Missions too,
Within her regions vast and broad,
And Ephraim, the backsliding Jew,
Shall soon stretch out his hands to God;
Then—then Messiah's reign shall come,
The knowledge of the Lord shall be
Spread o'er the earth 'till Nature's doom,
As spreads from pole to pole, the sea.

THE FOLLOWING LINES

WERE CALLED FORTH BY AN INCIDENT CONNECTED WITH THE BAPTISM OF TWENTY-TWO CONVERTS IN THE BEDFORD AVENUE BAPTIST CHURCH, BROOKLYN. THE PRESENTATION OF A BIBLE TO A YOUNG LADY BY THE PASTOR AFTER HER BAPTISM, AS A BEQUEST FROM HER FATHER, LATELY DECEASED.

THE pool of Bethesda's bright waters are flowing,
Oh come all ye sick and be plunged in the wave,
The "Master of Life" is rich blessings bestowing,
He waits in his temples almighty to save.

When earth was a void, and thick darkness enshrouded
The space which God's voice was to call into light,
The Spirit of God moved in brightness unclouded
O'er the face of the waters and banished the night.

And now like a flood the same Spirit is rushing;
Breaks down the dark barriers of doubt and of sin;
From hearts, hard as iron, the tear drops are gushing,
And group after group at God's altars step in.

Some seek for His grace in the baptismal waters,
"Like Peter" would lave "both their hands and
 their head."
Blest followers of Jesus! on these sons and daughters,
Be the gifts of the Spirit abundantly shed!

On one young disciple, whose sire had departed
But a few days before to the mansions above,
Did that parent bequeath to his child broken-hearted,
A precious memorial of fatherly love.

Oh take (said this dear dying saint to his pastor)
This Bible and give it, when I am gone home,
To my child, when in following our Heavenly
 Master
Through the baptismal waters she safely has come.

Oh! tell her that book was the guide of my life,
That in Death's chilling waters it comforts my heart;
May it cheer and support her through nature's short
 strife,
And bear her to heaven when she too shall depart!

Oh! may this bright season of soul-felt motion,
Be but the fair dawn of a still brighter day,
When the knowledge of God spreads from ocean to
 ocean,
And Millennium glories Christ's churches display.

LINES

ON AN ACCIDENT IN PRINCE'S BAY, OFF STATEN ISLAND, AUGUST 12, 1870.

I stood amidst a solemn crowd
In Tottenville's sweet rural shrine;
The organ peal'd a dirge aloud;
Each eye was dimm'd, each head was bow'd;
The stricken mourners shrieked aloud,
Not wails for *one*, but *three* combined;
Three fair young forms before us lie—
At *once* their spirits sought the sky!

One lovely girl, just budding fair,
Her mother's darling, father's pride:
A son, as cherish'd too, is there!
His manly beauty may compare
With her's, and good as he is fair,
Beauteous in death he lies beside;
His little brother's face is hid
Beneath the cold dark coffin's lid!

How died the three? Beneath the wave
They sank, with hands and arms entwined;

Their boat upset, none there to save
Too close the clasp the tremblers gave:
They rose not from their watery grave,
But one poor girl was left behind;
She saw them sink, she shrieked for aid;
Oh! why was it so long delay'd?

Alas! poor sister! mother! sire!
Two households plung'd in life-long grief!
God, help the mourners! lift them higher
Above earth's woes: let faith aspire
And give these sad ones sweet relief;
List to those voices midst the choir
Of angels 'round the throne above,
United in eternal love!

ON THE ASSASSINATION OF PRESIDENT LINCOLN,

APRIL 14, 1865.

WHY, Lincoln, was there no protecting shield,
No guardian angel to avert thy doom?
That to foul treason thou thy life shouldst yield?
A base assassin hurl thee to the tomb!

Just when bright "Victory" hovered o'er thy head,
And "white-robed Peace" proclaimed her advent nigh,
War's horrors drew not forth such tears we shed,
Such bitter tears, that *thus* our chief should die!

Oh! mourn Columbia, o'er thy tarnished name,
Where Freedom arm'd the Traitor's hand with *power*
With one base stroke to sully thy pure fame;
Thy fair Republic's most triumphant hour!

Four years, this day, the Stars and Stripes were lowered
From Sumpter's towers before a rebel host;
This glorious day, with joy they were restored
To the proud eminence which then they lost.

But as ordained to check all " human pride,"
To show the vanity of all below,
Our cup of happiness is dashed aside—
We lose our hero by a dastard's blow.

That heaven-born man, Columbia's pride and boast,
Next to our Washington, her noblest son
That upright, honest man—himself a host—
Slav'rys stern foe,.and Freedom's friend is gone!

Yes, he is gone! but to his country leaves
A noble heritage, a deathless name;
And now in heaven a golden crown receives,
Far, far above earth's highest meed of fame.

Nor do we mourn as those of hope bereft;
Tho' our Elijah has been called on high,
His spirit lives—his mantle has been left,
His memory and his cause shall never die.

ON PROFESSOR LOWE'S BALLOON ASCENSION NEAR RICHMOND, TO OVERLOOK THE REBEL FORCES.

In olden times when heavenly light
Was veiled from mortal eyes,
And he who caught a straggling ray
Was classed with deities.

When blind and erring man believed
In sorceries' witching power,
And bowed to gods of wood and stone
In sorrow's darkened hour.

Balak, the King of Moab, sent
To Midian's distant land,
To summon Balaam to his aid
To curse God's chosen band.

From Moab's high commanding hills
The Eastern Prophet gazed,
On Jacob's tents and Israel's host,
With awe divine amazed.

Enchantments could not dim the view
From his unwilling eyes;
His mental orbs saw Moab's fall,
And Israel's sceptre rise.

But what were Moab's rocks and hills,
To that astounding height
Where human science now can rise
And view Earth's warriors fight?

Above the clouds man now can soar,
Leave mountains far below,
And view but as a silvery line
The broadest rivers flow.

Lowe floats sublimely poised in air
O'er Richmond's fated towers;
Oh, may he see the star of peace
Above the storm that lowers.

Not far removed in heavenly space,
But fast approaching near,
When Freedom's flag shall proudly float
O'er this broad hemisphere.

ON THE DEATH OF MY MOTHER.

My gourd is withered!—she is gone
   Who most could wake my hopes and fears,
Of all beloved the dearest one,
   The dearest from my earliest years.

My mother! O, on that loved name
   How oft will fond remembrance dwell!
Earth ne'er can know a tenderer claim—
   A mother's fondness who can tell?

With what a sweet, seraphic smile
   Her mild, her gentle spirit fled,
So much like life, that for a while
   We scarcely could believe her dead.

So calm she looked, her lips apart
   Appeared as if about to move,
Some fond memento to impart,
   Some parting token of her love.

Yet, mother, would thy mourning child
   (Could she) recall thee here below,
Though then she cried, with anguish wild,
   "Spare me, O God, this trial?"—No.

ON THE DEATH OF MY MOTHER.

In mercy thou wert but removed
   From sorrows yet to come, and woe;
And, fondly as thou wert beloved,
   That very love would answer, No.

Farewell, dear mother! thou art blest;
   Thou slumberest with the peaceful dead;
And oft thy child, with grief opprest,
   Would lay by thine her weary head.

Farewell, till in a happier sphere,
   When earthly sorrows grieve no more
They whom the grave has severed here
   Heaven's opening portals shall restore.

ON THE LETTER O.

In gods and in demons 't will ever be found,
Wicked men it will shun, but in good men abound,
Yet on woman attends, as vibration on sound.
On the surface of ocean its presence you see,
And 'tis always contained in an old hollow tree.
In hot and cold countries 'tis destined to dwell,
On mountains, in forests, the anchorite's cell.
It never inhabits the halls of the great,
But a cottage prefers to grandeur or state.
With the Pope it however has always remained,
And in Rome has for centuries past been detained;
In the Catholic's claims it has openly stood,
Though in justice it aims at the general good;
It ever has proved the support of the crown,
In the Hanover line has been always passed down;
Our famed London without it would nameless become,
And its loss would be nearly as fatal to Rome.

ON THE VISION OF ST. JOHN,

DURING HIS BANISHMENT TO THE ISLE OF PATMOS.

  Thou, to whose favored view
  Heaven's portals open flew,
And visions bright of glorious things were given!
  Thou, to whose piercing ken,
  Unseen before of men,
The Saviour ope'd the golden gates of heaven!

  Beloved by him whose love
  No change could ever move—
No, not the dazzling change from earth to heaven!—
  He to thy ravished sight
  Disclosed his glories bright,
When, scorned by men, to exile thou wert driven.

  Vain Cæsar's vaunted power—
  Poor emperor of an hour!—
To banish thee from earthly courts of clay,
  When thy Almighty Friend,
  Before whom kings must bend,
Could bear thee to the courts of heavenly day!

ON THE VISION OF ST. JOHN.

  How mean thy purple robe,
  Proud tyrant of the globe,
Would seem, contrasted with the brilliant sight
   Of Jesus' glorious state,
   And all who round him wait—
Those countless hosts, arrayed in purest white!

  And are there here a few,
  To Jesus' precepts true,
Who, scorned by men, are yet beloved by Heaven?
   A little flock there is,
   Designed for heavenly bliss,
To whom Christ's love, to whom Christ's grace is given.

  John saw a countless band,
  From every clime and land,
Redeemed from among men, Heaven's presence fill;
   All clothed in robes of light,
   By Jesus' blood made white
In Calvary's stream, that fountain open still.

  In Christian virtues fair,
  They Jesus' image bear,
In spirit and in truth and heavenly love;
   Till, having left below
   All for his sake, they go
To join the hosts of his redeemed above.

ON THE MIRACLE AT MOUNT HOREB.

"Behold, I will stand before thee there upon the rock in Horeb; and thou shalt smite the rock, and there shall come water out of it, that the people may drink."—Exodus, xvii. 6.

GREAT is the Lord, and great his power!
   His mercy great—mighty to save!
On Horeb did his glory shine,
   Gushed from the rock the rolling wave.
At his divine, omnipotent command,
   His rod the prophet took—
O, wondrous act of the Almighty's hand!
   Forth issued from the flint a bubbling brook;
Nature the God of nature's fiat hears;
   What once seemed adamant, a stream appears.

His chosen people faint with thirst,
   A dreadful lingering death in view;
Exhausted in the wilderness,
   Their Maker saw, and pitied too.
Anguish, and pain, and deep despair
   Seized every tortured soul.

"Ye are the objects of my tenderest care;
  Fear not, my people!—be ye whole!
Smite thou the rock!" Jehovah said.
  A river flowed, as Moses prompt obeyed.

Type of that spiritual Rock
  Which after ages should behold,
From whence a stream should issue forth,
  Refreshing the chief Shepherd's fold.
That Rock was Christ—that saving stream—
  Was life, and health, and peace,
Which all his church derive from him;—
  That stream shall never cease.
"Smite thou the Rock," Jehovah said,
  And Pilate all unconsciously obeyed.

BRAY HEAD, WICKLOW.

TO MISS C. S.

Dear Charlotte! our ramble along the sea-shore,
When Bray Head's fair prospect we sought to explore,
    You beg me to give you in verse;
And, though no cold critics my lines may commend,
I ever comply with the wish of a friend,
    And thus our adventures rehearse.

'T was a bright, glowing day, in the dawn of the year,
When the primrose and violets begin to appear,
    And Winter seems struggling with Spring;
This day the fair youth seemed the victory to gain,
And dreary old Winter to give up his reign,
    And away his dark mantle to fling.

The air was as mild as a morning in May,
The sky was so bright, and the midges so gay,
    All nature appeared to rejoice;
The sea, and the waves, as they rolled on the land,
And sparkled, and dashed the white spray on the sand,
    Seemed to echo the general voice!

But, though all above us was brilliant and fair,
Though the sky was so clear, and so balmy the air,
    Yet some traces of winter we found;
For when Bray's rugged headland we sought to ascend,
On our most cautious footsteps we scarce could depend
    From the damp, slippery state of the ground.

But, mutually lending each other our aid,
We the summit attained, and were fully repaid
    By the prospect which greeted our sight;
Whilst below, 'midst the rocks, the sea eddied and boiled,
With the roar as of cannon, and fruitlessly toiled,
    As the waters were chafed in their might.

One false step, and our wanderings for ever were o'er,
And earth's varied beauties would charm us no more,—
    We should sink in the chasm below!
From the fearful abyss, then, our eyes let us turn,
To where Howth and yon minature isle we discern,
    And the waters so peacefully flow.

Perchance, my dear Charlotte, when hither you stray,
When your friend may be far o'er these waters away,
    You may think of your wanderings here;
And wherever that absent one's footsteps may rove,
Yet Erin's sweet shores and kind friends she will love,—
    They will still be to memory dear!

LINES TO ——,

A BEAUTIFUL BUT VAIN YOUNG LADY.

Your request, my dear girl, is a delicate task;
Pray what would you wish me to say? let me ask.
Must I tell you your eyes are of heavenly blue?
That your face and your features are beautiful, too?
Must I tell you all this? Nay, more, must I say
These serve but your sweetness and sense to display?
No! a flatterer might tell you all this, but a friend,
Believe me, will ne'er to such a meanness descend.

A beautiful person, we constantly find,
Is not always adorned by a beautiful mind;
And though a fair face admiration excite,
The effect it produces is transient and slight.
Disappointed we turn, with contempt and disdain,
From a form, though angelic, if heartless and vain;
But if mind and if heart correspond with the face,
To love and esteem admiration gives place;
'T is the wind which alone can illumine the whole;—
Beauty attracts the sight, but sweetness wins the soul.

THE MISSIONARY.

Go, messenger, from realms on high!
   On wings of love thy mission bear;
To earth's remotest regions fly,
   And plant thy sacred banner there.

The red cross wave o'er Afric's sands,
   And bid her swarthy natives know
Their great Creator's mild commands,
   And at the name of Jesus bow.

The red cross wave o'er India's soil,
   O'er Ganges' waters raise it high;
The Hindoo, worn with heat and toil,
   Shall to its grateful shadow fly.

The red cross wave where Buddha reigns,
   His idol temples overthrow;
Soon shall it burst his iron chains,
   Though forged by Satan's host below.

The red cross wave o'er Southern seas;
   Pacific! be thy islands blest!
Breathe soft, ye winds! Heaven's favoring breeze
   Speed gospel blessings to the West!

The red cross wave where Northern suns
    Scarce warm the earth, scarce melt the snow ;
Where life's dull current feebly runs,
    Scarce felt is nature's genial glow.

The red cross wave o'er land and sea
    From north to south, from east to west;
Let Father, Son, and Spirit, be
    Through all earth's varied nations blest.

PAIN AND PLEASURE.

How vain to look for happiness on earth!
Friends drop around us, even from our birth;
And could we be ourselves exempt from woe,
Ah! still the tear of sympathy must flow.

Yet, O, the tear of sympathy is sweet!
The painful heart-throb is with balm replete;
Pleasure and pain here ever are combined,
And tears give pleasure to a feeling mind.

Here, too, we cannot taste without alloy
Intense sensations of delight and joy;
Angels alone, the *heights* of rapture know,
And fallen angels feel the *depths* of woe!

Placed in a medium state, let us beware;
Heaven be our hope, and virtue be our care,
Pleasure encourage us our course to steer,
And pain still warn us what we have to fear.

ON SEEING SOME CHILDREN BLOWING BUBBLES.

SEE yonder youthful circle, blowing
    Bubbles high in air,
While their hearts, with mirth o'erflowing,
    Know no thought or care!

See the sparkling globules rise,
    Quickly in succession!
Some, ambitious, seek the skies,
    Some, yielding to depression,
One moment sink, the next to mount on high,
And end their wavering course more brilliantly.

Like visions glittering in life's young day,
    Bright as yon globules, like them light as air—
Like hopes by disappointment swept away,
    Which, vanishing, are followed by despair—
Like shadowy phantoms of the poet's brain,
    Or like ambition's wild-aspiring schemes,
Equally bright, and equally as vain,—
    Like fancy's magic, or like lover's dreams,
Emblems of all by which we're here perplexed—
    This world itself a *bubble* to the next.

LINES,

SUGGESTED BY THE DISTRESS IN IRELAND IN 1847.

O, Erin! how long are thy woes to continue,
    Are thy sorrows and sufferings never to cease?
Poor stricken one! say can no sufferings win you
    From the Father of Mercies an answer of peace?

Direct to yon cabin your pitying glances,
    See two youthful brothers are laid side by side,
One dead, and one dying—the pastor advances,
    And the rites of religion are calmly applied.

He dies! and the third who was patiently striving
    To give some relief to a fourth worse than he,
Sees him droop and die, whom they thought was reviving,
    And faints, and soon follows the first stricken three.

Oh! this is no fanciful picture of sorrow,
    Would God, that it were! but look yonder again,
See that tall manly youth from his mother's breast borrow
    The strength to encounter more hardship and pain.

Yes, mothers! behold that poor infant—look there!
  'T is deprived of the nourishment nature decreed,
That the just fainting son may be strengthened to bear
  The labor on which *the whole family feed.*

O, England! my country! withhold not thy hand
  From the famishing sons of affliction beside thee,—
While moved with compassion this far distant land
  With noble examples has richly supplied thee.

Poor Erin! thine isle like a *beacon* is shining,
  And prophecy's page is illumed by its light
That famines must come. Oh, then cease all repining,
  Bright days often follow a dark gloomy night.

Already from evil has good been extracted,
  Across the broad waters came help from afar;
Poor Erin! thy sorrows so deep and protracted,
  Have called to thy aid the American Star.

With the warm feeling hearts of a generous nation,
  Whose sympathies feel for the whole human race,
They rush'd to thy succor from every station—
  Oh! ne'er from thy memory their kindness efface.

SCENE AFTER A HURRICANE,

ON THE WESTERN COAST OF IRELAND—BOAT FREIGHTED WITH DEAD BODIES.

HARK! hear ye not the piercing cry,
   That doleful mourning, long and loud?
The echoing rocks and hills reply
   To the deep wailing of the crowd.

A boat appears! with outstretched hand
   And eager eyes her course they hail;
But scarcely does she touch the strand,
   Again resounds that mournful wail.

That boat contains a solemn freight
   Of human corses, lately glowing
With life and health, perchance elate
   With happiness o'erflowing.

Redeemed from the devouring tide
   The empty caskets now are borne,
Each to his own beloved fireside—
   Alas that *thus* they should return!

SCENE AFTER A HURRICANE.

The animating spirits fled,
    Ah! what avails the lifeless clay?
The piercing "keen cry" o'er the dead
    With empty sound shall pass away!

But let not thus the warning pass
    Which issues from their humble biers,
As many a warning voice, alas!
    Is heard with dull and death-like ears.

The winds repeat the solemn sound,
    The waters in each rushing wave;
Destruction both have scattered round
    And yawned hath many an early grave!

Full many a fabric man hath reared,
    One awful moment levelled low,
When to perform his will prepared,
    God bade the angry wind to blow.

It swept through nature's wide domain,
    The forest's pride were prostrate cast;
The growth of ages strewed the plain,
    Loud groaning in the ruthless blast.

But who can count the human souls
    That perished in that fearful gale?
When the last trumpet shakes the poles,
    It—it alone—shall tell the tale.

SCENE AFTER A HURRICANE.

When God's almighty power appeared
   In tempests bursting o'er his head,
The " still small voice " Elijah heard,
   As to his cave he trembling fled.

And shall not we, by mercy spared,
   While judgment thus has stalked abroad,
Be by such dread events prepared
   To listen to the voice of God?

That gentle voice, O, may we hear
   In the deep silence of the heart,
Dispelling all but godly fear,
   And bidding every sin depart.

WELCOME SONG TO JENNY LIND.

AMERICA, land of the mountain and lake,
  Of the storm, and the torrent's loud roar,
I have braved the wild waves of the deep for thy sake,
  And exult that I tread thy loved shore.
    America, land of the brave and the free,
    The home of the Pilgrims, thou'rt welcome to me!

I love thy bold rocks, and I love thy broad plains,
  Thy prairies and forests so grand!
And I love them the more, that within them there reigns
  The free soul of my own Fatherland.
    America, home of the brave and the free;
    The Minstrel of Sweden rejoices in thee.

Thy dawning was bright under Washington's star,
  But more glorious thy midday shall shine,
Thy sun has arisen o'er the nations afar,
  Nor till nature's last doom shall decline.
    America, land of the brave and the free;
    Meridian glory now smiles upon thee.

In Britain's proud halls, they have bowed to my
    strains,
  And success all my efforts have crowned;
But my calm Swedish soul uncorrupted remains,
  By the plaudits which echoed around.
        And I welcome the land of the brave and
            the free,
          For the home of the Pilgrims is dearer to
            me.

ON MUSIC.

Music, soother of the soul!
    Purest balm to mortals given!
Passion bows to thy control,
    Thy sweet strains partake of heaven.

Thou canst cheer the wounded heart,
    When depressed with earthly woes,
Comfort gently canst impart,
    Wildest feelings calm compose.

Joy wakes from thee a lovelier strain;
    Mirth with thee delights to dwell,
And, in sportive pleasure's reign,
    Lightly strikes the vocal shell.

But all thy noblest powers are joined
    To emulate devotion's flame;
With strength and harmony combined,
    Be this thy proper end and aim.

Seraphs golden harps employ
    To celebrate Jehovah's fame,
While the harmonious choir on high,
    Of spirits blest, resound his name.

When, in a melodious song,
    Earth echoes back the heavenly strains,
Angels the dying notes prolong,
    Sweet music fills the ethereal plains.

LINES TO A FRIEND,

ON HIS COMPLAINING OF THE INSUFFICIENCY OF PHILOSOPHY AS A SUPPORT TO THE MIND UNDER AFFLICTION, AND THAT HE MEANT TO SEEK THAT SUPPORT IN RELIGION AND THE SCRIPTURES.

O, SEARCH the bright record,—let nothing restrain thee,—
The earnest pursuit shall be crowned with success!
Let not earth, with its varied temptations, enchain thee,
Seek Him who alone can life's pilgrimage bless!

Can Science true happiness ever bestow?
Will Philosophy prove from fate's arrows a shield,
Or blunt the barbed shafts of affliction? Ah, no!
Its impotent arm in the conflict must yield.

Religion alone can the armor supply;
The shield must be faith, and the spirit the sword,
The breastplate of righteousness,—these may defy
The world, in the name of a crucified Lord!

O, seek then that armor,—prayer ever obtains it,—
　The Saviour has promised, "Ask, it shall be given;"
That promise how sacred! the Bible contains it;
　He reigns who has made it on earth and in heaven.

O, seek it in faith; with humility crave
　That wisdom which science can never supply;
That comfort and peace which the world cannot give,
　Nor with which the world's treasures in value can vie.

THE WAGER.

IN ANSWER TO A CHALLENGE FROM A YOUNG GENTLE-
MAN, IN WHICH EACH WAS TO WRITE TWENTY LINES
OF POETRY, WHICH WAS TO BE SUBMITTED TO THE
JUDGMENT OF FRIENDS.

A MINSTREL wreath I'm called to twine,—
Come, aid me, all ye sisters nine!—
  I've twenty lines to write;
A rival holds a tempting prize,
And my poetic power defies,—
  Come, gird thee for the fight!

No mean opponent hast thou found,
To meet thee on Parnassian ground;
  Shouldst thou the laurel gain,
And this fair company decree
The meed of victory to thee,
  Thou may'st be justly vain.

At friendship's call thou oft hast waked—
Here glory, honor, fame, are staked—
   Come, lady Muse, defend me!
Be thou my sword, be thou my shield;
The knight must to the lady yield,
   If thou wilt but befriend me.

Yet, should the wished-for prize be mine,
Or this just court award it thine,
   Yet when the contest ends,
Though poets seldom can agree,
The world at least *one* proof shall see
   That rivals may be friends.

A SKETCH.

I saw her in beauty, I saw her in pride,
   In life's brightest lustre, youth's earliest bloom,
When her cheek with the hue of that rose might have vied,
   That decks the green sod which encircles her tomb.

I saw her when, coloress, faded, and pale,
   That lily her delicate emblem might be;—
Or the marble on which is inscribed her sad tale,
   Warning others they may soon lie lowly as she.

I saw her encircled with each magic charm,
   With each witching spell, which earth has to bestow,
And I saw her shrink back in dismay and alarm,
   When death, hovering over her, menaced his blow.

I saw her when suffering had blanched her fair cheek,
   And her eyes, once so brilliant, now trembled with tears;
But a sweet, placid smile, and her accents so meek,
   Assured us religion had banished her fears.

In health's brightest bloom, she never had seemed
  So lovely, so beauteous, so heavenly, as now;
When her eyes and her smile with wild gayety beamed,
  And her pale cheek was flushed with a delicate glow.

I saw her as calmly she yielded her breath;
  The tear was now gone, but the smile still remained
On her beautiful features, when sleeping in death,
  Which no trace of her sufferings or sorrow retained.

L'INCONSTANT.

He saw, he admired her, and sought to inspire
   Her susceptible heart with love's sweetest emotion;
He strove to anticipate every desire,
   And silently paid her the deepest devotion.

He saw the deep blush he could call to her cheek,
   And vainly imagined the conquest his own;
Then heartlessly left her, fresh triumphs to seek,
   And exult in the victory he thought he had won.

But he knew not the spirit of womanly pride
   Which, though sweetness itself, she could call to her aid;
She summoned it now, and successfully tried
   To forget the impression his falsehood made.

He saw, and too late, with remorse and regret,
   That she viewed him with feelings allied to disdain;
He felt that, like him, she could learn to forget,
   And ne'er trifled with woman's affections again.

SELF-EXAMINATION.

While darkness shrouds thy mortal sight,
In nature's solemn stillness, night,
These questions to thine heart apply,
And let it answer honestly.

What have I done that I should not?
That which I should have I forgot.
Have I done aught to mark my way,
Or, like the Roman, lost a day.

Have I thought what I fain would hide,
When my heart's inmost depths are tried?
Or said what I should blush to appear,
When God, and man, and angels hear?

Have I employed my tongue in praise
To him whose mercy crowns my days?
Or thought of Him who gave me power
To think, that I might love him more?

A day is added to my store,—
Who much receives should render more;
Since yesterday another given,—
To-day am I more fit for heaven?

LINES ON THE DEATH OF A YOUNG LADY.

Mourn not for Marg'ret! her sufferings are o'er,
  And her glorified spirit rejoices in bliss;
Triumphantly crowned, she remembers no more,
  In the joys of the next world, the sorrows of this.
Conformed to her Saviour in suffering here,
  She drank of the cup which her Father had given,
And exchanged, for a higher and holier sphere,
  The trials of earth for the treasures of heaven.

Mourn not for her, though in youth's early bloom
  The summons to leave all most dear has been sent;
Though tears, bitter tears, may be shed o'er her tomb,
  He loves her far more who recalls what he lent.
Yes, Marg'ret! in thee I have lost one whose love
  Through life I had hoped would my pilgrimage cheer;
But though thou hast fled to the mansions above,
  My trembling footsteps may follow thee there.

Mourn not for Marg'ret! though great be our loss,
  Though her sweet disposition endeared her to all;
If we strive for the crown, we must take up the cross,
  Else earth would our wayward affections enthrall.
Though cold is that heart which so warmly could glow,
  Though silent that voice which so sweetly would thrill,
Though the sigh may arise, the unbidden tear flow,
  We would bow to the stroke most submissively still.

ON THE DEATH OF THE DOWAGER LADY POWERSCOURT.*

Angels, strike your harps of gold!
    Who surround the eternal throne;
Though the Godhead ye behold,
    Sympathy with man ye own.
O'er his fallen, yet kindred, race,
    Still ye watch with holy love,
And, ransom'd through a Saviour's grace,
    Behold him seek your ranks above.

Hail ye now a happy soul!
    From our world of woe and care,
Lo! she gains the blissful goal,
    Comes your heavenly joys to share,
Through the portals of the grave,
    In the steps her Saviour trod,
Who in death the victory gave,
    And conveyed her home to God.

---

* This pious lady had felt a presentiment of her approaching death a week before she was attacked with any sickness, and immediately arranged her affairs, o the most minute particular, accordingly; on completing which, she was aken ill, and died in a few days.

DEATH OF THE DOWAGER LADY POWERSCOURT.

Clothed in garments pure and white,
    Cleansed in Calvary's crimson flood,
Sinners! who (in robes so bright)
    Comes to view her Saviour, God?
She who gains a heavenly crown
    Earthly honors meekly wore,
Gladly laid the burden down—
    Powerscourt was the name she bore.

Wealth was hers, but she had learned
    Where alone true riches lie,
And from worldly treasures turned,
    Seeking those beyond the sky.
Early doomed to feel the smart
    Of affliction's chastening rod,
She reposed a widowed heart
    On the bosom of her God.

Through this wilderness she passed,
    Supported by her Saviour's arm,
And to behold his face at last
    Could death of every sting disarm.
Hastening her duties to fulfill,
    Assured her Lord would call her home
From that high station which his will
    Said, " Occupy till I shall come,"

Her stewardship she calmly closed,
   Though yet no sickness touched her frame;
Her house in order she disposed,
   And then the looked-for summons came.
She sickened,—human aid was vain,—
   She *knew* that *now* her hour was come.
Angels, pour fourth a glorious strain!
   Her happy spirit welcome home!

METRICAL LETTER TO MISS N——.

My very dear Friend:

In your absence I send a few lines to remind you of those left behind you. I hear that to Derry you journeyed quite merry, and your brother to greet you had hastened to meet you; to whom, by the way, I my compliments pay, with his friend and your own, now no longer unknown, for ere this, I dare say, they have stolen you away from the town and its noise, to the country's sweet joys. Apropos to your city, my heart throbbed with pity, as I yesterday read, in the history by Reid, of the right noble stand of the patriot band, by whom in the siege Londonderry was manned. Such sufferings and zeal, to our feelings appeal, and make Derry shine bright in fair virtue's sweet light.

It surprised me to hear, that her walls still appear, complete as they were in that notable year, their breadth though so great, such strength might create, as might cause them to last to so distant a date. O my dear, to look down on the river and town in so sacred a spot, must not every thought be with past recollections of chivalry fraught? No wonder your mind caught a tone more refined, and the scene which you drew bore so vivid a hue!

But, as my vagrant Muse no such prospect now views, she must beg you her errors and faults to excuse. And, wishing you every joy and delight, and hoping (when leisure permits) you will write,

   My dear Mary Ann,
    • Pray believe me to be,
     Sincerely affectionate,
      Yours, — F. E. B.

A SKETCH OF CONNEMARA,

A ROMANTIC DISTRICT IN THE WEST OF IRELAND.

Come, my friends, in fancy climb
Binnebola's heights sublime!
See their frowning summits vie,
Proudly towering to the sky.
Now behold yon darkening cloud
Their stately majesty enshroud;
Now dispersed and chased away
By the sun's enlivening ray.
Soon emerging to the view,
Clothed with every varied hue,
Chameleon tints of green and blue.

Now turn we where fair Clifden stands
And many a pleasing scene commands;
But no description can convey
How picturesque her church and bay;
Nor can we greater justice do
Her castle and its beauties, too.
But come all ye who love the roar
Where wild, impetuous torrents pour;
See that frail bridge sustain the shock
Of waters dashed from rock to rock.

Collecting from the neighboring hills,
The flood the very arches fills,
And, foaming down the craggy steep,
Forms eddying whirlpools vast and deep.
Yet here the daring trout can leap,
And darting through the foam and spray,
Unharmed pursue their venturous way.
But see, in treacherous mazes set,
Yon fisher throws the wily net,
And cautiously conceals the snare
Beneath the rock, with jealous care,
Just where the angry waters boil,
And thus secures the finny spoil.

To Roundstone now our way we take,
O'er mountain moor and lonely lake,
Where the wild-fowl rear their broods,
In these romantic solitudes.
O, that the food, earth, sea, and sky
For man's subsistence here supply
By starving thousands were enjoyed,
Who of these comforts are devoid!
O, that these vast unpeopled plains,
Where so much native beauty reigns—
Neglected spots of Erin's isle—
Were decked with culture's cheerful smile!
But I must hasten to conclude

My rambles through these regions rude,
Lest I my kind friends' patience tire,
A prospect which I don't admire.
But should they on some future day
Again desire with me to stray,
Perchance my humble Muse once more
May Connemara's wilds explore.

TO A FRIEND,

ON HIS LEAVING ENGLAND FOR SOUTH AMERICA.

If aught can urge a friend's request
    With more prevailing force,
'T is parting thus from east to west,
When meeting must involve, at best,
    Uncertainty, of course.
Yet think not I would damp the zeal
A sailor's breast should ever feel;

For British bards have sung that zeal
    In music's richest strain,
And British hearts must ever feel
How strongly to their love appeal
    Her wanderers of the main;
Then go, and prosperous gales convey
Thy bark upon its destined way!

Yet think, while o'er the trackless deep
    Thy vessel smoothly glides,
Or should the angry billows leap,
And rise in watery mountains steep,
    Who o'er the storm presides;
Remember Him whose sovereign will
Can bid the winds and waves be still.

Yes, Edward, yes; the voyage of life
    Demands a sailor's care;
Passions, the elements of strife,
And rocks abound with dangers rife,
    All unsuspected there;
Mists blind our eyes, our track pursue,
And hide our wished-for port from view.

The Bible is the compass given
    By which our course to steer;
When tossed by billows, tempest driven,
" A pilot to the port of heaven "
    Points with directions clear—
He who once trod the briny wave
To prove his mighty power to save.

TO A YOUNG LADY DURING SICKNESS.

My gentle Jane, accept a willing lay,
    An honest tribute most sincerely penned
No empty compliments I mean to pay,
    But simply breathe the wishes of a friend.

Perchance the muse may prompt a serious strain,
    As one best suited to a suffering hour;
But soon may'st thou both health and strength regain,
    Nor feel the sad effects of sickness' power.

Yet think, dear girl, while yet it pleases Him
    (Who chastens whom he loves) your faith to try,
Who calls for clouds the youthful eye to dim,
    That earth's vain scenes may pass less dazzling by;

Who summons pain, or sickness, or distress,
    To show the emptiness of all below,
To teach fond man that He alone can bless,
    That lasting peace from Heaven alone can flow.

Oh, think of what makes even sickness blest,
    Without which health and earth's best gifts are vain,
Which gives to life's true joys their purest zest,
    And renders death itself eternal gain.

I wish thee all which this world can supply,
   I wish thee health, and happiness, and ease;
But all that's bright must fade, that lives must die—
   Then, oh! dear Jane, I wish thee *more* than these.

I wish thee endless life beyond the tomb,
   Pleasures that *never fade*, nor joys that fly;
Leaves "for the healing of the nations"* bloom
   In that blest land, on trees that never die!

" And in the midst of the city was there the tree of life, and the leaves of the tree were for the healing of the nations."—Rev. xxii. 2.

LINES FOR AN ALBUM.

TO MISS A. S.

ALICIA bids me wake the lay,
    Alicia courts my muse;
Sweet girl, with pleasure I obey,—
    'T were painful to refuse;

For well I feel, though weak the strain,
    Though poor the lines may flow,
No critic harsh have I to gain,
    Approval to bestow.

Alicia loves the simplest proof
    Of friendship and regard;
To gain her smile were boon enough
    To inspire a worthier bard.

But much I fear her poet's lyre,
    Though tuned with earnest heart,
Can never equal or aspire
    To half her painter's art.

LINES FOR AN ALBUM.

No flowers have I of hue so bright
    As his, to adorn the page;
No brilliant tints to attract the sight,
    And pleased regard engage;

Else should the rose of England twine
    With Erin's shamrock green,
And friendship's ivy-leaf divine
    Bloom verdantly between.

THE THREE AGES OF HUMAN LIFE.

CHILDHOOD, careless age, farewell!
    Thy scenes have passed away,
And it makes the heart in my bosom swell,
While thus I sing thy parting knell,
    And think of thy joyous day.

Youth, thou art speeding on thy course,
    And art gliding swiftly by;
Each hour augments the rapid force
With which, like a torrent from its source,
    Thy rapid moments fly.

Age, with the silver locks, art thou
    Destined my fate to mark?
Cheerless and sad thou seemest now;
Thy withered cheek and thy wrinkled brow
    Unlovely are and dark.

Life, thou art ever changing, still
    Fleeting from goal to goal,
With the stealthy pace of a trickling rill,
For eternity's boundless sea, to fill
    Thy fair, but fragile, bowl.

LINES

SUGGESTED BY READING THE FOLLOWING ACCOUNT OF INSTANCES OF BRAVERY AT THE DEFENCE OF A MEXICAN BATTERY AT VERA CRUZ:

["At the Mexican battery, which fought so well, when the flag-staff was shot away, an officer tore the flag from the remnant of the staff, jumped upon the parapet, and held it in his hand, until he himself was shot down. This was done three times."]

STANDARD of Mexico fall'n from thy glory,
    Yet wert thou grasp'd by a Patriot hand;
Brave hearts of ev'ry clime, hear the sad story,
    Mourn for his fate through Columbia's land.

The flag of his country, before the invader,
    With anguish he saw was just ready to fall;
" My country!" he cried, and sprang forward to aid her,
    Snatch'd the flag, and once more it wav'd high o'er the wall.

The flag-staff was shatter'd—he flung it aside
    And held the torn emblem of freedom on high;
" Oh! on, my brave soldiers," he fearlessly cried,
    " With this let us live, or with this let us die!"

Once more from the battery a volley resounded,
  And every shot carried death in its track;
Columbia's bravest gazed on them astounded?
  But soon their bold fire, with dire sweep echoed back.

Down dropp'd the brave Mexican shot through the heart—
  The banner was steep'd in his fresh flowing blood;
But not with *his* life did the spirit depart
  With which, as a martyr, he nobly had stood.

Another was found on the instant to stand
  In the place where he proved as a mark to the foe:
He fell too!—yet still a third stretch'd forth his hand
  To grasp the lov'd banner, and then be laid low.

Columbia's standard now proudly floats o'er
  The once beauteous city of fair Vera Cruz;
But when shall war's triumphs be echoed no more,
  Which each faithful Christian most painfully views?

Oh! when shall the clarion no longer be heard,
  And these contests and strifes between brethren cease,
When shall man—proud man—bow to his Lord's written word,
  And the reign of Messiah be hallow'd by peace?

ON THE DEATH OF A FAVORITE CAT.

Gentlest of the feline race,
Pet of our domestic hearth,—
Long we'll mourn thy placid face,
Purring song and playful mirth.

Seven long years thy faith we tried,
Favorite of our house and home;
How we'll miss thee from our side,
How regret thy mournful doom.

Our returning steps to greet,
Thou would'st frisk the room around,
And, with light and nimble feet,
O'er the chairs and tables bound.

Or the market basket smell,
With sharpened scent for morsels rare
For thy instinct knew full well,
Poor pussy's dinner would be there.

Honest as the canine race,
Besides the viands thou wouldst sit
With air demure and patient face,
Nor 'till 't was given thee, touch a bit.

Yet, though gentle as thou wert,
No mouse dare near thy precincts come,
Or no precaution could avert
From him the hapless felon's doom.

Thy milk-white fur so soft and sleek
Would, with keen anger, quickly rise,
And, tigress-like, thy prey thou'dst seek,
And fire like flash thy amber eyes.

Thy sympathies, poor puss, were all
To nature true—a mother's love,—
Brood after brood of kittens small,—
Thy faithful tenderness may prove.

Oh! had'st thou died by nature's stroke,
Had age, with gradual sure decay,
Thy senses dimmed, thy life-thread broke,
We might have seen thee pass away

With less regret, though not with eyes
E'en then unmoistened with a tear;
But ah! poor puss, a sad surmise
Afflicts us, that thy short career

Was shorter made by human means,
Which bade thee yield thy parting breath;
That poison rankled in thy veins!
And caused thy sufferings and death.

ON THE DEATH OF A FAVORITE CAT.

We've laid thee in a quiet space,
Where forest trees will o'er thee wave,
And spring's first vedure mark the place
Which holds poor pussy's humble grave.

There shall our footsteps often turn,
And memory on our favorite dwell,
Our hearts with love and pity burn;
Alas, poor pussy, fare thee well.

ON THE BAPTISM OF AN INFANT.

Creator of the human race,
    Almighty Father of mankind,
I humbly bow before thy face,—
    O, may my child thy favor find!

Saviour! obedient to thy word
    I bring my infant son to thee;
Accept and bless him, gracious Lord!
    Say, "Suffer him to come to me!"

Baptized with water all must be,
    According to thy plain command,
And cleansed by sovereign grace, as free
    As water poureth through the land.

Baptized in the most sacred name
    Of Father, Son, and Holy Ghost,
O, may my son thy mercy claim,
    And gain the grace by nature lost!

My cherub boy, thy infant smiles
    Bring gladness to thy mother's heart,
Which many a painful thought beguiles,
    In which thy future fate hath part.

But He who loved thy helpless race,
   And clasped them fondly to his breast,
His providence thy wants embrace!
   On this thy parent's hope must rest.

He can through life thy wants supply,
   In death, his mercy still can save,
On cherub's wings can make thee fly,
   And bear thee safe o'er Jordan's wave.

TO A FRIEND

FOR CHRISTMAS DAY, 18—.

Accept this trifling mark of love!
Affection's hand its meshes wove;
May "silken cords" as closely twin'd,
Our *hearts* and *souls* together bind!

May heaven its blessings on thee pour!
Thy purse contain a golden store,
And love and truth, those *gems divine*,
More *bright* than *gold*, be ever thine!

But all earth's treasures still must fade!
The true, the loved—be lowly laid;
Then be thy surest riches stor'd
In brighter worlds, with Christ the Lord!

This day, we hail his heavenly birth;
This day, a babe he came on earth.
Forsook the glories of the skies,
To win for man the "heavenly prize."

Then may *we* lay up treasures there
In heaven's blest courts, so bright and fair!
That world of peace and joy above,
Eternal as the Saviour's love!

ON THE BIRTH OF AN INFANT.

Welcome, my darling, to thy mother's heart,—
A gift from God, a precious trust thou art;
A soul, confided to thy parent's care,
To train for heaven and Christ's blest mansions there.

Like Moses, in his ark of reeds and mud,
Thy fragile bark floats on a troubled flood,
Launched on the waves of this world's stormy tide,
More dangerous than Egyptia's waters wide.

But the same God who interposed to save,
And snatched him from the Nile's o'erwhelming wave,—
That providence, which Pharaoh's daughter sent,
And to her heart his tears made eloquent

His fate o'erruled, and He whose word can save,
Caused her to draw him from his watery grave
And take him for her own,—that Hebrew boy,
Whom cruel Pharaoh's mandate would destroy—

That providence, my babe, can shelter thee
From all the storms of life's tempestuous sea,
And bear thee safely to that happy shore
Where all its waves and storms can reach no more.

TO ANNIE.

Though dark be the season of dreary December,
   A wreath we may pluck from an evergreen tree,
And when Erin's kind daughters I fondly remember,
   A garland I'll twine, my dear Annie, to thee.
The ivy, revealing of friendship the feeling,
   The holly of Scotia's famed bard shall be thine;
While mistletoe blending, its elegance lending,
   For thee, my dear Annie, a garland I'll twine!

And though far away soon my footsteps may wander,
   And the banks of the Foyle I no longer may see,
Full oft on the friends far removed shall I ponder,
   And my thoughts shall revert, my dear Annie, to thee!
Or should music, soft stealing o'er each tender feeling,
   And touching the chords in fond memory's shrine,
Full oft on each note, thy remembrance shall float,
   And the voice of its numbers, dear Annie, be thine.

AN ACROSTIC.

FOR AN ALBUM.

J oyfully I court the Muse,
A nd wake for thee the votive lay;
N or thou, dear maid, the boon refuse,
E ntreating which my vows I pay.

E steemed, and honored, and beloved,
L et me, dear Jane, thy friendship claim;
E ager to have these lines approved,
A nd prizing naught like thy sweet name,—
N o, not a word thy tongue can frame,—
O , smile upon my simple lay!
R eceive my vows this festive day.

P rizing a world of bliss above,
O , may thy years on earth be blest!
P romoting all which Christians love,
E ternal be thy happy rest!

HYMN.

O'ER the dreary waste of waters
   Where my dear one's footsteps roam,
Father! be thy care extended!
   God of mercy and of love!

As of old, almighty Saviour!
   Bid the winds and waves be still;
Now, as then, the powers of nature
   Wait upon thy sovereign will.

Spread your shelt'ring wings around him,
   Ye whom heaven's blest mission bear.
Holy angels, guardian spirits,
   Take, O, take him to your care!

Still this fallen world ye visit;
   Though unseen, his steps attend;
Viewless messengers of mercy,
   From all ill his course defend!

And when life's short voyage is over,
   When the waves of Jordan roll,
O, may angels round him hover,
   Heaven's blest shores receive his soul!

ON THE ANNIVERSARY OF MY BIRTHDAY.

God of my life! another year
  Of that short life is past,
And this for aught that I can tell
  May be decreed at last.

As wave is urged on wave,
  Year after year rolls by,
Bearing me ownward to the shores
  Of bright eternity,

Eternity, or wished,
  Or feared, must come;
Beyond earth's narrow bounds
  Is placed our home.

Whether the golden bowl
  Unbroken shall remain,
Whether the silver cord
  Its links unsnapped retain,

Till nature yield
  To time's all-powerful sway,
And the tired spirit gently quit
  The tottering clay,—

ON THE ANNIVERSARY OF MY BIRTHDAY.

Or whether, ere the charms
   Of life are fled,
The fatal shaft of death
   Lay low my youthful head,—

Is only known to Him
   Who reigns above,
But who extends to all
   A father's care and love.

Whether the coming year
   Be doomed to be
A year of peace and joy,
   Or fraught with misery,

I know not, and 't were vain
   For me to know
What portion I'm assigned,
   Of joy or woe.

He who the sparrow's fall,
   Deigns to decree,
Yet rules the monarch's fate,
   Will care for me.

He, to whose piercing eye
   A thousand years are one,—
He will appoint my lot
   And mark my span!

He *will* appoint ?—he *has*,
　　Ere time began;
E'en *I* was not o'erlooked
　　In Heaven's bright plan.

The meanest child of earth
　　May—must—sustain
Some one connecting link
　　In Time's great chain.

He in his wisdom planned
　　My course through life;
He saw if I should fall
　　Or conquer in the strife.

He knows the soul he formed,
　　He hears each feeble prayer,
Which, when to Heaven breathed,
　　Finds entrance there.

He knows the heart he framed,
　　Each feeling ere it rise;
He sees each struggling tear,
　　He hears its sighs.

He knows each blessing's worth,
　　He know's each trial's power,
Sustaining strength imparts
　　In sorrow's hour.

Through every scene of life
  His guardian care extends,
Nor with this fleeting breath
  His kindness ends.

For, when the fluttering pulse
  And closing eye,
In the last mortal hour,
  Call man to die,

If in this lower sphere
  He has performed his part,
Fulfilled his Maker's will
  With single heart,

He bears his spirit hence
  To realms above,
Where it will flourish in the beams
  Of everlasting love.

In his protecting care
  May I confide,
And all my future life
  O, may he deign to guide!

LINES TO AN OLD SCHOOLFELLOW.

My dearest Elizabeth, at your desire
   I exert my poetical vein,
And if not the muses, let friendship inspire,
Although not a spark of the radiant fire
   Of genius embellish the stream.

We've been children together—now childhood is past
   The spring-time, the dawn of our years,
'T is gone! and our summer will vanish as fast;
O, let us remember that youth will not last,
   Nor sigh when grave autumn appears!

We've been school-fellows, playmates, companions, and friends;
   May time our affection improve!
May we rival each other in laudable ends,
While, matured by experience, our judgment commends
   Our early attachment and love!

Companions are numerous, friends are but rare,
  True friendship but seldom is found;
'T is a delicate plant, must be cherished with care,
Requires showers and sunshine, warm soil and pure air,
  While fenced and well guarded around.

The soft tear in sorrow, the bright smile in joy,
  True friendship must ever bestow;
Sincerity pure and unmixed with alloy,
While firmness must guard, lest the cold world destroy
  The heartfelt, ennobling glow.

The cold world—ah! yes, my dear girl, 't is indeed
  Cold, heartless, and dangerous, too;
From its snares and temptations, O, may we be freed!
Its frowns may we brave, with heaven for our need,
  When we bid it for ever adieu.

www.ingramcontent.com/pod-product-compliance
Lightning Source LLC
Chambersburg PA
CBHW031343160426
43196CB00007B/728